BORN AND

Portraits of St Ives

ANN KELLEY

CORNWALL BOOKS

First published in Great Britain in 1988 by Cornwall Books

ISBN: 1 871060-06-0

British Library Cataloguing-in-Publication Data
CIP Catalogue Record for this book is available from
the British Library

Printed and bound in Great Britain by Penwell Ltd, Callington,
Cornwall for A. Wheaton & Co. Ltd, Exeter.
CORNWALL BOOKS
An imprint of Wheaton Publishers Ltd. A Member of
Maxwell Pergamon Publishing Corporation plc

Wheaton Publishers Ltd
Hennock Road, Marsh Barton, Exeter, Devon EX2 8RP
Tel: 0392 74121; Telex 42794 (WHEATN G)

SALES
Direct sales enquires to Cornwall Books at the address above.
Trade sales to: Town & Country Books, P.O. Box 31, Newton
Abbot, Devon TQ12 5XH. Tel: 080 47 2541

DEDICATION
*To the memory and in celebration of the life of my son, Nathan Kelley,
who died aged twenty-four following a heart and lung transplant.
His great spirit and laughter live on in our home in St Ives.*

ACKNOWLEDGEMENTS
Thanks to all the people of St Ives who agreed to be part of my book. However, making a book and achieving some sort of balance means that some important people had to be left out: Thank you Betty Ralph and Charlie Ninnis for the lists of family nicknames. Thank you John Barber for allowing me to use the Shamrock Lodge verse. Thank you to all my friends who helped select pictures. Thank you to my husband Robert Marshall whose loving support helped me finish the project.

Special thanks to Dr Roger Slack for the tape recordings of St Ives people from which the text is taken. His generosity has given my images of the present their connection with memories of the past.

Thanks also to John Smith for providing the prints for use in this book.

FOREWORD

As I was going to St Ives, declares the old riddle, *I met a man with seven wives*. No town in Britain is a more appropriate host to the septigamist, because it is a place of many identities. It is the glowing sapphire, catching the breath as its bay slides into sight on a sunny day. Such days are not common enough anywhere in Cornwall; yet in my experience one can often catch at least a haze of sun in St Ives when the skies everywhere else are leaden. 'Let's try St Ives,' we say, when drizzle soaks us; and even if the drizzle doesn't relent, there is usually a lighter, hopeful patch of cloud, which slightly lifts the spirits. So one St Ives is a creature of hope and illusion, poised on the edge of unreality, as it is in Virginia Woolf's *To the Lighthouse*.

St Ives is also the cheap-and-cheerful resort of amusements and chip-baskets, fudge-shops and pacamacs. It's the town of solid hotels and guest houses, moneyed and unromantic. It is a bohemian town of artists; they are drawn by the magical light, and by the grey, silent stony magic of the Penwith moors. St Ives is like a bright clasp on a sombre cloak, but it is still a part of that cloak, a part of the moors; one can see it in the surrounding mine ruins, and in Barbara Hepworth's sculptures. You know you are not far from the ultimate point of Britain, that the north and the south coasts are running together, running out.

There is the tough, working-class town of fishing — now largely of the past; and of struggle against the sea — still very much alive, as evidenced by the lifeboat-station. And underlying *this* St Ives is a close-knit, proud, rather secretive Cornish community, threatened by the more recent identities of the town and by the loss of its traditional work, yet miraculously surviving. Ann Kelley records an astonishing richness of nicknames, passed from generation to generation of old St Ives families; when you next visit the town, seek, as you suck your icecream, My Honey, Coochie Fadge, Dick Worm, Bessie Wet Tits, Dashing Billows, Katie Fashions, Katie Cut Cock, Nancy Kangaroo and Billy Ole Times: they're around, but you won't find them. The nicknames are revelations of wild Celtic humour and the need to block out the stranger.

Sevenfold St. Ives. You could have a wife in each town, and they might never meet...

Ann Kelley has no nickname, she is an adopted daughter of St Ives. But over a quarter of a century she has taken it to her heart, and – to judge from her photographs – the town has returned the compliment. It is not always easy to persuade 'ordinary' – that is, almost always extra-ordinary – people to let you take their photograph; there lurks the primitive, and rather healthy, belief that making an image of you steals your soul. But the shining characteristic of Ann Kelley's photographs is that she doesn't do this. There is nothing meretricious or flamboyant in her art; she is concerned solely with recording the truth. Her portraits of a fascinating town and its people have a rare integrity. Her subjects have trusted her, and she has not betrayed their trust.

D M Thomas
Truro, 1988

CONTENTS

INTRODUCTION

This collection of portraits is a thankyou to St Ives, which has been my home on and off since 1962. My children went to school here, played in back lanes and rock pools and walked the cliff path to Zennor. We have made lifelong friends here.

Obviously the town has changed over the years, sometimes for the better, sometimes not. The old fishing community has almost disappeared, but you can still find a few survivors smoking a pipe and telling a yarn, or keeping the adrenalin flowing over a stormy game of euchre or dominoes in Rose, Shore Shelter or Shamrock Lodge. Their children, grandchildren and even great grandchildren are still living and working in St Ives, and family nicknames are handed down from one generation to the next. There's a strong feeling of community and family which rubs off on us 'foreigners'.

Some things don't change. Wind rattles the sash windows and gulls scream; the white sound of sea is always there. Locals still greet each other in the old charming way – 'My lover, my handsome, my maid, my cock, my bird'. Children still play in our back lane twenty years after their parents played with my children.

Ann Kelley

Windy Day at Porthminster

TOWN

Then we used to be washing. Used to go out Carthew, on the rocks to dry the clothes, with great plaskets of clothes, on the rocks. Then you're watching the sea, 'fraid the sea's coming in to them. But we generally know the tides. Then you have to go out pick them [the clothes] in.

ANNIE WILES

Father was a wall mason. Mother was Italian, hence my middle name. She was a lady's maid for Mrs Dow up at Talland. My grandmother reared me. She was from a fishing family. The whole family was fishing. Didn't know anything else. The worst thing they did in my estimation – to the fisherfolk that were down here – why they did it I don't know, but they said 'condemned' and put them up in the council houses. I call it the 'reservations'. Funnily enough the same fishermen's cottages are still in existence and still in use. Didn't make sense. So what you've got now down here are no longer St Ives people. Very, very few. And as they die so someone else takes over the property, not a local.

CHARLES ANGELO NINNIS *(born 1914)*

St Ives from Trezion. The roof of the Zion Congregational Church.

Washing on the wharf

I never missed school, except once when a crowd of us, it was such a lovely day and we missed because we wanted to go swimming. And the whippereen, he was called Jackson; you would call him the man that come round when you stay away from school. Well, the whippereen, well there was a crowd of us sitting down in front of the Sloop [Inn] waiting for our bathing costumes to dry, and he give us all a good dressing down. And of course I had a row with my father and wasn't allowed out for a week. But I did go out. Mother used to send me out, 'go to Miss Johns's.'

We used to go to the dances up at the Palais when Hill had the Palais then. And Saturday afternoons used to be pictures. *Pearl White* was the serial and the other one was *The Green Archer*. And we used to get our ticket and not get it torn, and used to go around outside and if any other girls or boys had no money to go in, we used to give them that ticket. But we used to go to the dances for sixpence with refreshments. And we have gone from Malakoff, when the buses started, to the Prince's Pavilion in Falmouth for two shillings and sixpence, dance and everything. We've had some good times.

BETTY RALPH

Used to go down on the wharf, down on the quay, see the boats going off to the North Sea, down there shouting 'Bring home a pair of garters for us, mind, don't forget the garters'. Happy times we've had down there. Lovely times.

Used to be all full of vessels down there you know, when you used to go down over Dick's Hill, used to look down, used to be all boats — big boats, small boats, different boats, lovely. Now it's all gone. Lovely old times.

ANNIE WILES

All the small shops had boxes of salt-fish, piled up boxes in front of the door. I can remember all the dogs coming along and lifting their legs on the fish!

ROBERT CARE *(born 1907)*

4

Smeaton's Pier

Illuminations

Above Clodgy

Barnoon Gospel Room (Plymouth Brethren)

Misty Morning, St Ives Harbour

St Ives from Porthminster

Extra busy time then. Everyone who had a horse, from Lelant this way, from Zennor this way, was pretty well engaged this time of the year, pulling the fish with the carts. Pulling the fish. Now, forty, fifty thousand herring used to be a common occurrence then and they're all counted up then by hand, in threes. The women used to have to go down and count them out the gurries. They would say – a 'score'. Well, a score would be about forty-one threes, wouldn't it? Always the odd three. Hundred and twenty, hundred and twenty-three. Always very . . . Oh, I would like to see it again, Oh 'es, like to see it again.

HENRY TREVORROW

Used to have the Fair Mow* in the Green Court, what is called Tregenna Place now. Used to do all the aunts' errands and we had sixpence; we had a lot of money to go up Fair Mow. So we used to go up and buy a brush, it was made of string with the wire end, and one of these balls on elastic, and a skeeter, a skeeter that we used to 'skeeter' people. It was a tube like a lead tube filled with water. Mother used to say, now bring the brush home, because she used to clean the chimneys of the lamps with this brush, and she would take some fine tissue paper and put the polish on.
    And we used to go round the aunts and do errands. Otherwise we never used to visit them. We'd have sixpence for this Fair Mow. And there used to be all carbide lamps outside. They used to buzz. All up around the Green Court and by the library there used to be Fair Mow. And you'd get a bag, used to call it Cornish fairings, a bag of gingerbreads, a piece of angelica, and lemon biscuits and macaroons, all for half a crown.

*Fair Mow = *Fair Mogh* (Pig Fair)   BETTY RALPH

The old habit of the St Ives people in the lower town washing down the streets and all the little lanes on a Saturday night – it's all finished. The Fore Street, after the fish had been going up, through and up Tregenna, well, that was all washed down by the town on Saturday night. Sunday morning the town looked beautiful.

CHARLES ANGELO NINNIS

SEA

I was born 1907. I've lived in St Ives all my life, born and bred. Come from a fishing family. Been fishing all my life since I was fourteen, bar when I went yacht skipper out of Southampton 1934. I stood that till the beginning of the war. That was the done thing then. There was plenty of private yachts then. There was money in that business.

My father, he and his brother had a boat between them – the *Tiger*. She was a small boat but she was a good getter. In the herring season she was one of the top boats. Then my father he had a gig afterwards – the *Cutty Sark*. I sold she after my father died in 1933. Things were very very bad then. You couldn't get a living. You could catch fish but you couldn't get no price for them.

At one time there was seven hundred fishermen in St Ives. Not like it is now. I went fishing at the age of fourteen. I was trawling most of the time till I finished. During the war and after you could get a very good living, though the price of fish was controlled. It's an occupation. If I had my time to go over again I should still do it because it's a carefree life and more or less no bosses. You only got tide times. It's a marvellous life if you like the water.

ROBERT CARE

Brothers Sam and Eddie Bassett mending nets on Smeaton's Pier

John Stevens of Beach Road, St Ives. Fish merchant of St Ives Fisheries;
Member of Cornwall County Sea Fisheries Committee;
Chairman of Cornish Fishing Vessels Insurance Society Ltd;
Member of the Committee of the United Fisherman's Co-op Society Ltd;
Owner of Trawler *Girl Rene*.

Matthew Stevens, fish merchant from 1947. Father and grandfather were fishermen.
Four generations of Matthew Stevens all lived in the same house, 59 Fore Street.
The painting, by Brian Jay, shows Matthew and his son Matthew in the
family business in Back Road, St Ives.

Paul Michael Turner of the Old School, Lelant. Electrician by trade and Auxiliary Coastguard. Formerly a Sergeant in the Royal Marine Reserve, and cliffman in Rescue Team.

We was nine boys and a sister, Sarah. And my mother reared two nephews as well, Dan and Kenneth. So we was eleven boys altogether. We lived down the Bluebell. Father was a fisherman and pilot. He was Edward Charles. He had six boats then. He had three boats of the herring fishing – *Bluebell*, *Maggie Ann*, and *The Reaper*. And he had two sailing yachts. We used them for pleasuring. And then my brother bought another sailing yacht. That was before they brought in the modern launches. It was half a crown for two hours fishing and sailing. They were the summer days like you used to have.

When I was a boy, once you finished work – down the rowboats or in one of the yachts, or in a boat trip round the lighthouse or to Gurnard's Head. That was before Seal Island was invented.

GASCOIGNE PAYNTER *(born 1912)*

You know that old skill, that I've seen Tom 'Paddy' – Tom Pearce – and one or two of the older men, watching for a shoal of mullet, that old skill is gone. He taught me and I went out to Clodgy and there was a whole load of local lads there with rods, 'There's no fish here,' and I was looking down on them. And they all cleared off so I rigged up my rod and fished away and caught quite a few. But they couldn't see the things. It's a dying art.

CHARLES ANGELO NINNIS

Gascoigne Paynter of Bethesda Hill, St Ives.
*'I do all the signwriting for the lifeboats. Jim Pearce the painter and
decorator used to do them boards. The father died and the son took over.
The son died and I took over.'*

Thomas Cocking, 1987. Lifeboat Coxswain from 1967 – father, Thomas Cocking,
was a lifeboatman and grandfather was coxswain from 1928–1939, when he was drowned.
Son, Thomas Cocking, is lifeboat mechanic.

Henry Plummer, retired painter, decorator, and fund collector for the RNLI.
Each year he displays his oil paintings of seascapes and lifeboats in his front garden at
Ayr Terrace. With him is Penroe, 'the fastest dog in Cornwall.'

Harry Barlow, retired coastguard of Knill Cottages, Steeple Lane.

Jack 'Meor' Veal, retired fisherman of Bailey's Lane, and
John Paynter, boatman, of Bowling Green Terrace.

Martin 'Danny' Roach of Beach Road,
Wharf Bosun of Trinity House and Flight Marshall of Trinity House.

We fished for herring, pilchards, mackerel, ling, lanyon, conger, cod, ray, turbot, skate, the lot. You had to go in the channel for that. Had to go ten or twelve legs (leagues, you'd say), for that. Used to be lots of skate around then. I can remember one time, aboard the *Tiger*, we went down off Round Island, down Scilly, and we loaded her down cellar, right down to the bends with line fish. And we had a stiff breeze, a south-easterly breeze come up. And we was given up for lost. We was twenty-four hours overdue, and I can remember tipping the oil out of the dang lamps to get us home. And when we come in there was a crew of men on the quay waiting to take over to moor her, and we all went home. We was all wet through cos we had a solid beating coming up. And the next day, the weather was so bad we couldn't land the fish in our punt. It had to be pulled ashore by line. And the skate wouldn't sell, and we had to go out and dump the skate. We couldn't get nothing for the skate. You could get a ling for sixpence then. Rays was eighteen pence, half a crown a stone, something like that. You couldn't get no money for fish then.

I can remember my father, I believe it was my first trip as a boy. He lashed me against the lampstandard forward. We had no pump. I don't know what would have happened, cos she was loaded down, anything could have happened.

ROBERT CARE

Then the pilchards went. Well, I think after the last war the Italians wasn't buying no pilchards. And the drift business started to fail and in the end the pilchard season died off altogether. The only one buying pilchards now as far as I know is Shiphams and they're all catched by trawl. There's no drift nets now, nowhere. And a trawl kills off everything in time.

I've seen it years ago – foreign trawlers coming home from The Smalls loaded down to the beds with herring. Well, we used to reckon the herring used to spawn around The Smalls. Well, they was trawling. The herring went. You could only get herring during the wars when trawling was stopped. Since then it's dried up completely.

How many smoke houses were there here then? There was Rogers, Brown, there were four or five different kippering houses here then, smoke houses. Saturday nights the town used to be full of smoke.

When the herring season failed, everything failed.

ROBERT CARE

HOME

I can remember my grandfather Care fishing because he went fishing with my father then. But old Will my other grandfather, he was ninety-four when he died, but I can never remember 'e fishing, now I think he was a seafarer. He must have done fishing too. But he was a bit of a character really. He used to wear a stetson hat. Beard, something like Buffalo Bill. But he spent more time in the Sloop than anything else, and I think there was nine children, I think my mother was one of nine. Course they're all dead and gone now.

ROBERT CARE

Doctor R. Didn't like ee. Wouldn't have ee for the cats. Great tall man he was. And he lost a young woman who was a visitor to here. He left her too long. Then he started to work, my dear, all her ins — all her everything — was coming down over the bedroom stairs. Was like a butcher's shop. She was a lovely young woman. It was her first baby. He didn't have many patients after that. The town took against him. Big rough man, he cleared out after that. Oh, I couldn't take ee. I didn't like the look of him.

ANNIE WILES

The old people, all of them had a cat, because the loft door had a cat hole in. The idea was if you had a cat in the loft you had no mice. And if a mouse got in a bundle of nets, by the time you came to use them they'd be like crochet — big holes and small holes.

CHARLES ANGELO NINNIS

Betty Ralph of Trerice Place, worked for many years for
the family of the painter Peter Lanyon. She tells great yarns.

Eliza Trevorrow of The Digey, St Ives.

Beryl Pollard, mother of four children and member of the Salvation Army.

Zoe and Dickie, the 'Singing Postman', Stevens outside their home in The Digey, St Ives.

Willie and Alice Care outside their home 'The Doll's House', Back Road West.

Frank and father, Dick Perkin, masons, at Frank Perkin's home in Carnellis Road.

'Young William' – William Bennetts in Virgin Street where he lives with his sister,
and their dog, in the house where his parents lived.

Symons Family at Trenwith House, Trenwith Lane, January 1986.

UPSTAIRS, LEFT TO RIGHT
Jackie the Mynah bird, David Symons (Mark and Judy's son);
Rebeccah Symons (Christopher and Jane's daughter); James Symons (Christopher and Jane's son);
Charles Symons (son of Timothy and Moira);
Paul Symons (son of Roger and Shiela); Timothy Symons and mother Moira.

DOWNSTAIRS BACK ROW, LEFT TO RIGHT
Roger, Shiela, Maurice, Mark, Judy, Christopher, Timothy.

FRONT ROW
Floss, Sue Baker, Alison, Henry, Hannah, Jane.

I was born in St Ives in the Digey and lived in this cottage since I was three. When we moved to the house I'm in now there was no water outside. We had to go with a pitcher to a public tap. There was no electric or gas. We had a oil lamp in the kitchen and a candle or a small oil lamp to go to bed with.

There was no flush toilets. Every night people emptied their bucket down on the beach to dispose of that.

CHARLES ANGELO NINNIS

The period from Christmas until April or May, that was the dead season. In that season you had the salt herring. You had a pig's head cut in half and that was put in brine. In the autumn when there was plenty of rain they would go off and buy plenty of butter and wrap each pound in cheesecloth and put that in brine. There was a lot of stuff salted in those days to carry you through that bad spell. That was where the potatoes and bread came in. You needed it.

But nobody starved.

CHARLES ANGELO NINNIS

I was brought up on spuds and bread. If you had a meal, even if it was a sheep's head boiled with broth: 'Have a maw' – the old people didn't call it a slice of bread – 'that'll help fill up the crevices.' Even if you had a salt herring and potatoes boiled in their jackets: 'Have a piece of bread to fill up the holes'.

CHARLES ANGELO NINNIS

It's not St Ives now. We was one big family you know. If there was anyone ill they would say, 'Who is going to stay up with Bill or Sarah tonight?' And they'd have a cart-load of sand outside the cottage to deaden the sound of the horses and carts.

WILLIAM CARE

Douglas Paynter, one of Gascoigne's eight brothers, at
home in Alexander Place where he builds model boats.

WORK

This was a hard place for working fish you know, because the sea was out and horses used to go down, men used to go down, getting in the gurries. Otherwise, if the water was in all the time they could have got them in on the quay like they do in Newlyn. Get about eight hundred fish in a gurry, and sometimes they'd be aground out in line with the two [pier] heads, and the buyer who bought them maybe on West Pier, and there may be forty gurries aboard that boat. And the men who carried they would carry the forty gurries, would be two men, would carry them right up around the sand, right up across the prom, drop them on West Pier. And while he's doing that, these crowd would be singing out: 'When you going to bring ours up?' They used to have sixpence a gurry for carrying them. They was strong men.

HENRY TREVORROW

Counting the herring. Getting your apron ready the Monday, 'fraid as a soul you weren't going to have dry weather to dry your check apron to count up your fish. Used to be happy times, lovely times.

ANNIE WILES

Hart's Ice Cream Parlour.
LEFT TO RIGHT: Vivian Hart, Bertha Hart (wife to Sam Hart),
Joyce Hart (wife to Phil Hart), Edward Hart, Pamela Hart,
Mrs Lillian Burrell, 'Teeny' Bunn(?), FRONT: David Bray.

William James Woolcock, 'Gremmy' of Dunraven, Higher Tregenna Road.
Beach proprietor of Porthgwidden and Porthmeor Beaches since 1980.
Gremmy played rugby for Cornwall, and has been a policeman and a lifeguard.
His father, William Pearce Woolcock played rugby for England Schoolboys
and was manager for Slades of Hayle.

Vivian Eddy of Tregwarry Road, with Snoopy Highflier.
Antiques dealer of Corner Antiques, Chapel Street,
Viv comes from a large family of brothers who make up a good
part of the cricket team of Gulval.

Norman Gale of Carbis Bay, Butcher. Member of St Ives Rotary Club and
Chairman of the Friends of Trewartha House (psychiatric and geriatric home).

Jane Furneaux of Jane's of St Ives, Cakes and Pastries,
renowned for her miniature 'Cameo' cakes.

N.R. Phillips, plumber, writer and ornithologist, Bard of Cornish Gorsedd and
winner of 1987 Peninsula Prize with his novel *The Saffron Eaters*.

Used to do pilchards – marinated fish. The man used to come from Newlyn every morning: 'Ullo. Ullo. Want some pilchards?'

'Es, want some pilchards. How much are they a hundred?'

'Half a crown a hundred.' ('Halfpenny each they were then!').

'Put two hundred down the cellar and I'll clean them directly.'

We had a great big cellar under the studios. After we've had breakfast, we've cleaned them. Have a great big pan under the tap, tap running and then another thing here to put them all to leak. Empty fish baskets on top to go over them. Take a great while, mind, a lot of work to do them nice.

Clean them all and strain them all, cut the tails off and scale them you know, with a penny, and then take them off and put them under water. Tons of water we used. Then we take them up, put them on sink, leave them to leak. Left to leak from eleven o'clock till six or seven in the evening. Then we put them in the pan, layer after layer. Used to look lovely. Then used to put a bay leaf on top, then vinegar. Tie them down they great pots with brown paper. Carry them down to bakehouse. Left in all night then, see. And then seven o'clock in the morning we'd have people here knocking on the door, 'Are the malliows ready?'

ANNIE WILES

I was down the Holmes kipper house, cos we had to work when father was on the Corporation. First I started carrying bread in my school hours. I was working, woman was called Mrs Jenkyn. I used to get a shilling a week wages and sixpence for doing my work so well. So I used to give my mother the shilling and she used to tell me to keep the sixpence. I used to carry bread all around Porthmeor Road and I used to come home. What it was to do in the house? And my job was to clean the brass.

And I used to go to the Post Office to get a form to put penny stamps on, and when you got twelve penny stamps you would get a Post Office book. Then she used to say, if you got fourpence and you save threepence use the penny, but if you don't want anything, save the penny, don't squander it. And that's how I started saving. Of course, if you got a Post Office book with twelve penny stamps on you was a good worker and saver.

Mrs Trenbath of Gurnard's Head Farm.

R.H. and J. Rowe, Chy an Chy from 1966–86.
LEFT TO RIGHT: Jane Perkin, Alison Rowe, Richard Rowe, Joan Rowe.

Flower seller outside the main Post Office in St Ives

Monica and Margaret Lander, sisters, cat lovers and
hairdressers of 'Margaret's', Chapel Street.

Margaret Williams, housewife and mother of Trelawney Road.

We was all boat-minded. But, the five youngest of us, as we left school, father said, 'Now, here's the fishing boats. Now when you leave school, you learn a trade. It's up to you, but if you don't learn a trade you go fishing.' So Henry David, he was the first to leave school, he went masoning. William, he was the second one to leave school, he went carpentering. I was third, I went painting and decorating. Freddie was next, he went plumbing. Douglas was the youngest one, he went electrician. But all of us, after we left work we was always down the boats, either fishing or sailing.

As I say, you're sea-minded, you know. You combine it with your trade. The saltwater's in your blood.

GASCOIGNE PAYNTER

Mother used to work for Mrs Griggs a complete summer. When the summer holidays were on, me and my mother moved down to Tremedda Farm. I used to always wonder how she managed with that big open fireplace because she used to cook under those kettles in that big open fireplace. The grub was good though. I used to often wonder how do you know when it is cooked because it was covered with a piece of gorse, you know, furze, but she always seemed to know. She put it in a dish and was covered over with an iron kettle and the fire was put around it. But she had to have a sweet in one and meat in another, but it was all done. I remember this very well because you could go and sit in by the side of the fireplace and see daylight right up to the top.

CHARLES ANGELO NINNIS

Peggy Hendy Veal, eighty-one year old owner of The Albatross (also known as Hendy's) fish and chip restaurant in Chapel Street. The shop has been in the family for seventy years and Peggy Veal started work there when she was fourteen. Her father also had a wet fish shop in Market Place for fifty years.

YOUTH

As a boy the thing we all hated was Mondays. That was washday. That was the worst day of the week. Going to school and washday. We had to get in a traw [trough], a great wooden traw had to be brought in. The water had to be brought in. Was soapsuds all day long. When we come in to dinner all we had was 'et-ups from the day before, which was Sunday. And was bluin' mixed up, was starch being mixed up, and the last thing that was done was scrubbing the rope mats, cos everyone then had rope mats, the men going to sea and that, brought home rope mats. Course, there weren't no washing machines then, it all had to be done by hand. Our mothers must have had quite a stink.

ROBERT CARE

My mother had to go out to work, naturally. My grandmother reared me. When I came in dinnertime, midday, from school, very often, first job, 'Fill my needles'. That was the needles she'd used mending the net which was hanging on the mantleshelf. After I finished the needles, 'Now wash your hands'.

Another day I might come in and she'd taken the dinner (because the little fireplace had a little oven, and a little tank on the other side for to fill up to have a bowl of hot water). They'd have taken the dinner into the public bakehouse to be cooked. And I've landed home for dinner, and they'd given me a white flour bag that had been washed, and tuppence. 'Go on in the bakehouse and fetch the dinner'. You went in and asked for the dinner. You covered it over with the white flour bag and you give him the money and you brought it in. And by the time you'd got in my grandmother had washed the pickle off her hands or whatever the nets were done by, barked or pickled, and dished up the dinner.

Sixty year ago there was always a net hanging up to mend. Everyone was busy.

CHARLES ANGELO NINNIS   49

Edwin Andrews of Gill an Creet plays for St Ives Youth Band.

John Andrews, and twin brother Stephen, trombone players
of St Ives Youth Band, outside their home at Gill an Creet.

Jenna Woolcock, with Gordon the Gopher on Porthmeor Beach.

Karen Williams as Miss Piggy at the St Ives Junior School Book Week, 1987.

Claire Jenkin of Barnoon Villa, with Athena.

Cousins Naomi Perkin and Claire Jenkin outside Barnoon Villa, West Place.

Andrew Phillips, postman, son of N.R. Phillips, writer.

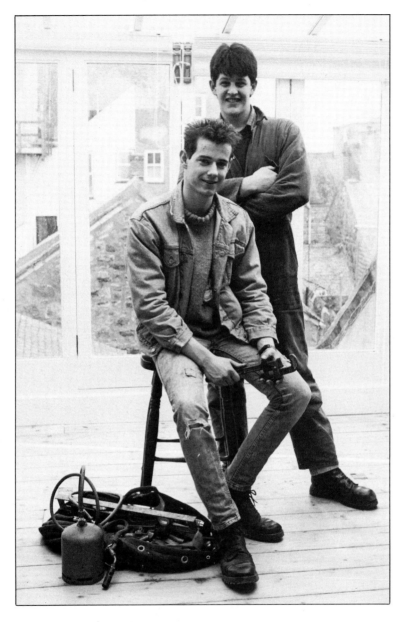

LEFT: **Mark Easterbrook Ryan of Hayle, plumber with H. Symons, St Ives. Won the Apprentice of the Year for the Southwest Award, 1985.**

RIGHT: **Kevin Veal of St Ives. Works for H. Symons. won the Apprentice of the Year for the Southwest Award, 1987.**

Amanda Cox and baby Daniel.

Our life was hard I suppose, and yet we had an enjoyable time. Gramophones then come out but we never had one. There was no wireless or television, but we had plenty of times at night. Well, we used to tip people's dust buckets up at night. The dust used to be collected every day with a horse and cart. And another idea was to tie two doors together with a piece of rope and have a stone on one and let go. One of us would knock at the doors. Now, neither one could get out, you see. I seen that done lots of times, specially with Tommy Rio, you didn't know 'e, he was an old chap lived up Island Road, top of Fish Street. He always wore a bowler hat. He was a funny old character.

ROBERT CARE

I can remember we. Oh, I was eleven or twelve year old then. There was a circus and menagerie coming up Trelyon. There wasn't no houses up there then, only a farm. All we crowd had no money. We never had tuppence to scrape bread with. Anyhow, a gang of us went up there. All the cages was covered up with tarpaulins. And we was going to see those animals somehow. Anyhow, we got in under a cage, taking turns to look up. And under a lion's cage, the chap that went last — he was down the lodge yesterday, funny enough, Edgar — anyhow, he said, 'I can see 'en, he's right up above me.' And exactly as he done that the lion let go. And the chap had a brand new jersey on. By God, his mother said, 'You can't wear that no more.' You see, he was right under the lion. We boys were tickled we pink. No doubt about it.

ROBERT CARE

LODGE

In my boy's day I used to see, as I thought, a lot of old men sitting in front of the Friendship Cellar. Well, they was all smoking, most of them. They had clay pipes then, of course. I thought they were old men but they must have been about fifty or just over. They all used to rise up when the mackerel boats were coming in. Go out the Island and watch the mackerel boats coming in. Where they got the money from for the baccy I don't know.

ROBERT CARE

The rest of the crew in my boat are all dead and gone. Nobody I sailed with are living at the present time. Now I was aboard the *Tiger*, they're all dead and gone. I was aboard Pett's boat, they're all dead and gone. I was aboard the *Freeman*, they're all dead and gone. I was aboard the *Cutty Sark*. They're all dead and gone. I was aboard the *Bluebell*, Andrew's boat. They're all dead and gone.

There were five hands on *Tiger*. Was my father; was my uncle, was two; Dan'l Coutts, was three; was Mr Hodge was four; was me, five.

ROBERT CARE

Edgar Humphries, retired painter and decorator, of White Hart Flats,
The Wharf, St Ives, in Shamrock Lodge, October 1985

Donald Williams 'My Honey', retired fisherman, in Shamrock Lodge.

Dominoes in Rose Lodge.

LEFT TO RIGHT: Peter Stevens, retired carpenter of Trewyn Flats;
Thomas Lander, retired fisherman of Bedford Road;
Steve Allen, mason's labourer, 18, Street an Garrow;
J.W. Stevens 'Johnny Tant', retired fisherman.

THE SHAMROCK LODGE

If these old walls could only talk what stories they would tell,
What stirring memories revive, and tragic ones as well;
With interludes in lighter vein, good fellowship and cheer.
A worthy breed those tough old salts who once assembled here.

I look around the little lodge at faces like my own,
Well furrowed by the scars of time as they have older grown;
And pensively reflect that we old timers of today,
So recently, in retrospect, were tiny tots at play.

They found a need for such a place, where fishermen at night,
All through the hours of darkness till the dawn of morning light,
Could come and go to meet their crews, and then and there agree,
To either give the night a miss or take their chance at sea.

At first they built a shelter from some oddments crude and cheap,
Discarded gear no longer fit for service on the deep;
A boat's old sail, a bench or two, a lugger's broken mast,
And soon they had a refuge from the cold and wintery blast.

Then somebody suggested how much better it would be
To build a more substantial place, and charge a little fee
To buy a cosy bogey stove; then members, day or night,
Could meet and have a bit-a-chat, all comfy snug and tight.

The council blessed the project and good naturedly agreed,
A tiny token charge for rent would meet the civic need;
They then assured the fishermen there was no cause for fear
If they would only guarantee one paltry bob a year.

Though oft by poverty impelled to plough the angry deep,
And face the hazards of the night while others lay at sleep,
One old tradition they revered, and nothing would induce
Our fishermen to compromise nor suffer its abuse.

The Sabbath was a special day for worship set apart,
The scriptures clearly said so, and the Bible was their chart;
And painted on the Shamrock wall for one and all to view,
A grand old Cornish motto renders, 'Meor Ras Ma Dew.'*

*(Great thanks to God.)

JOHN TUCKER BARBER

Enoch Thomas of Ayr Lane in Shamrock Lodge. Retired
mason and member of The Plymouth Brethren.

John Barber 'Johnny Tucker' of St Peter's Street. Song
writer and author, Bard of Cornwall since 1956.

Willie 'Bish' Care, brother to John 'Bish' Care. Retired fisherman, author and storyteller. Wrote 'Three Score and Ten'. Lives at Fernlea Terrace, St Ives.

Henry Symons, retired plumber, fisherman and farmer
with Floss in Shamrock Lodge.

John 'Bish' Care, retired fisherman and merchant seaman,
with a broken teapot in Shamrock Lodge.

Henry Perkin, retired fisherman and Charles Ninnis,
retired fisherman, airman and postman in Shore Shelter.

THIS THE 'SHORE LODGE' TOGETHER WITH THE 'ROSE LODGE' WERE ERECTED IN THE
YEAR 1918 AT THE REQUEST OF THE LATE SIR EDWARD HAIN KT. WHO BY HIS WILL
BEQUEATHED THE SUM OF £300 TO DEFRAY THE COST OF THE CONSTRUCTION OF
THESE TWO LODGES FOR THE FISHERMEN OF ST IVES.

Sign in Shore Lodge   67

Brothers Thomas and John 'Jewa' Stevens in Shore Shelter.

John 'Jewa' Stevens and Jack 'Meor' Veal in Shore Shelter.
John Stevens worked for the St Ives Corporation and lives in Virgin Street.
Jack Veal was a fisherman.

Phil Rouncefield, secretary of Rose Lodge, of The Meadow, St Ives.

Appendix

NICKNAMES

The tradition of nicknames in St Ives is worthy of deeper study for they form a lasting part of the cultural history of the community. Though the tradition remains strong, with names being passed from generation to generation, they will inevitably disappear, eroded by the tide of change.

Below are listed the nicknames attributed to the Stevenses, as recalled by Charles Ninnes. The second list recalls nicknames of families throughout St Ives, as recalled by Betty Ralph and told to Dr Roger Slack. In each case the nickname is written as it is pronounced locally:

Nicknames of the Stevens of St Ives

Christian Name	Nickname	Christian Name	Nickname
John W	John Jewa	James	Jimmy Roundy
John	John Selver	William	Willie Pessey
John	Jan Dykes	William	Willie Sailor
Richard H	Johnny Tant	William J	Polly Wassey
Richard	Dick Worm	Mathew	Mathy Gentry
Richard	Dick Fing	Mathew	Mathy Fake
Richard	Richard Chillray	Mathew	Mathy Paraffin
Richard	Dick German	Mathew	Mathy Spry
Richard	Halibut Dick	Louie	Louie Pett
Edwin	Edwin Gull	Thomas	Tommy Tilda
Job	Joe Powerful	Thomas	Tommy Poe
George	Dick Salt	Thomas	Tommy Blue
George	George Tea Leaves	Earnest	Brookham (Conchie)
George	George Trawl	Paul	Captain Starve Guts
George	Georgie Pupteen		
George	Georgie Happi	Robert	Bob Cush
George	High George	Sam H	Doctor Tibbles
James	Jimmy Lemputs		

Nicknames of St Ives familes

Nicknames	Surname	Nicknames	Surname
Mikey Nuna	Abrahams	Jimmy Lemputs	Stevens
Traulee Foot	Uren	Georgie Shirs	Baragwanell
Horn		Stewed Mackee	Veal
Sia	Nichols	Peter Hotbark	Veal
Edward La	Stevens	Pint 'n a Pennard	Trevorrow
Whisper	Grenfell	Raundee	Stevens
My Honey	Williams	Billie Bunkin	Davies
Mathy Crust	Freeman	Henee Puddee	Trevorrow
Atee	Edwards	Little Turtle	Trevorrow
Franky Flip	Nichols	Bobtails	Phillips
Tommy Noggin	Toman	Rinclaw	Richards
Coochee Fadge	Couch	Pet	Stevens
Robby Ite	Wedge	Dashing Billows	Perkin
Hunchee	Williams	Muller	Trevorrow
Tommy Tilda	Stevens	Smut	Curnow
Willie Country	Peters	Dick Fing	Stevens
Dick Worm	Stevens	George Trawl	Stevens
Gabo	Nichols	Dinks	Care
Emma Jewel	Hosking	Mena	Care
Paw	Stevens	Tibbles	Stevens
Biscay	Phillips	Peggy Blue	Cothey
Mary Ca	Gribble	Catern	Trevorrow
Bessie Wet Tits	Stevens	Walter Starling	Richards
Nancee Gannett	Andrews	Fat Maggie	Cocking
Paddy	Pearce	Ole Will	Bennetts
Tilly Toots	Stevens	Henry Guffa	Williams
Pancho	Samson	Sligs	Bennetts
Gull	Stevens	Dick-Shan-Hero	James
Mousie	Paynter	Tom Tabee	Noall
No Cocky	Uren	Johnny Bowls	Peters
Tripey	Pearce	Jan Dykes	Stevens
Flap	Berriman	Janny R Charles	Paynter
Snash Nee	Veal	Annie Joa	Stevens
Lizzee Long	Humphries	Helen Duddles	Uren
Ben Higgins	Phillips	Bob Cush	Stevens
Farthings	White	Willie Black Dog	—
Happy Dick	Jones	Mary Annie	
Dickie Admiral	Farrell	Brightwork	MacEwen
Clara Buw	Nichols	Monk	James
Annie Duck	Jennings	Katie Fashions	Baragraneth
Dick Shitty	Veal	Sandy	Care
Nubs	Veal	Philip Ayr	Paynter
Lizzie Cock	Curnow	Mathy Paraffin	Stevens
Mabya		Froggy	Peters

Nicknames	Surname	Nicknames	Surname
Pad-an-Arf	Perkin	Billy Blue Nose	Veal
Mary Boo She	Cocking	Mary Ann Glem	Pertreath
Tommy Red	Care	Smiler	Lander
Mary Bood	—	Pupteen	Stevens
Georgie Bunnee	Ninnis	Shelaw	Perkin
Johnny Luggars	Ninnis	Antnee Tadlee	Couch
Uckernasher	Taylor	Gordie	Andrews
Dick	Stevens	Bessie Urn	Trevorrow
Willie Pessey	Stevens	Jack Fen	Thomas
My John	Cocking	Dick Gaymo	Perkin
Mikey Tinsee	Taylor	Dick Shoe	Stevens
Willie Bumps	Williams	Peter Slipree	James
Yanks	Williams	Battle Axe	Williams
Polly Wassey	Stevens	Lizzie Coddles	Care
High George	Stevens	Sanko	Bosanquet
Jack Furl	Farrell	Nickie Tight Ass	Paynter
Shiloff	Hodge	Pick Pockets	Care
Mathy Fake	Stevens	Sally Trotters	Uren
Katie Cut Cock	Peters	Jimmy Stingbum	Stevens
Scran	Peters	Uncle Uss	Bennette
Shill	Peters	Snuff	Murt
Bessie Two Thumbs	Freeman	Ole Voo	Cocking
Parkey James	Richards	Tom Puffer	James
Georgie Bealtee	Uren	Benjy Poop	Penberthy
Johnny Mallet	Care	Dack	Hart
Mary Ann Mackee	Care	Mossee	Taylor
Jimmy Shealer	Mitchell	Mackie	Trevorrow
Mary Moodee	Penberthy	Puggee Daw	Rowe
Mockie	Paynter	Pinhooks	James
Susie Buzz	Pollard	Nancy Kangaroo	Andrews
Sammy London	Ninnis	Bar	Cocking
Sailor	Stevens	Chit Chat	Mitchell
		Billy Ole Times	Matthews